A Million Little Dinosaurs

A million little dinosaurs
Having a good time –
One fell off a cliff
And then there were
Nine hundred and ninety-
nine thousand,
Nine hundred and ninety-nine.

Nine hundred and ninety-
nine thousand,
Nine hundred and ninety-
nine dinosaurs
Having lots of fun –
An asteroid hit the Earth
And then there were none.

Other fantastic poetry collections from
Scholastic:

Silly Poems
Disgusting Poems
Magic Poems
Animal Poems
Pet Poems
School Poems
Spooky Poems
Funny Poems
Funny Poems for Christmas

For more details about Paul Cookson,
visit www.paulcooksonpoet.co.uk

Dinosaur Poems

Compiled by
Paul Cookson

Illustrated by
Sarah Nayler

SCHOLASTIC

For Stuart, Dawn and Rob

*Special thanks to all the staff and pupils at
Wesham C.E. Primary School, Wesham, Preston.*

Scholastic Children's Books,
Euston House, 24 Eversholt Street
London NW1 1DB, UK
A division of Scholastic Ltd
London ~ New York ~ Toronto ~ Sydney ~ Auckland
Mexico City ~ New Delhi ~ Hong Kong

Published in the UK by Scholastic Ltd, 2006
This collection copyright © Paul Cookson, 2006
Illustrations copyright © Sarah Nayler, 2006

Copyright for individual poems is given on page 108, which constitutes
an extension of this copyright page.

10 digit ISBN 0 439 95174 7
13 digit ISBN 978 0439 95174 6

All rights reserved

Printed and bound by Nørhaven Paperback A/S, Denmark

1 2 3 4 5 6 7 8 9 10

Papers used by Scholastic Children's Books are made from wood
grown in sustainable forests.

Contents

Miscellaneousaurs

Dinosaur Remains

Last Word

Acknowledgements

Creature Features

The A to Z of Dinosaurs

All R eXtinct – **Z**zzzzzzzzzzz

Pam Gidney

– Er!

Watch Out!

The mighty acanthopholis
Had a diet quite specific,
It fermented plants in its giant tum
And its trumps were megalithic.

Roger Stevens

The Pterodactyl

The pterodactyl has a silent P
(Not just when no one's looking).
He's very difficult to spell
And rather tough for cooking.

Pam Gidney

The Dinosaurs

They lived on our planet before there were people,
Forebears of our reptiles and fishes and birds,
They were not called dinosaurs then – they were
  nameless.
They lived on our planet before there were words.

Some were as tall as a four-storey building.
To keep themselves going, they needed to munch
The green things around them from dawn until
  twilight –
Their waking existence was just one long lunch.

Some preferred flesh. They would tear at their dinner
With terrible fingers and teeth sharp as knives.
Others grew horns, massive spikes, bony armour,
To ward off the carnivores, safeguard their lives.

They all disappeared and the world went on turning.
We humans evolved, with our language, our games,
Our hunger for knowledge. We found the lost
  creatures.
We dug up their bones and we gave them their
  names.

They stand in museums; grand skeletons, relics
Exhumed after millions of years in the ground.
And we are still learning. Who knows what strange monsters
Lie buried around us and wait to be found?

Wendy Cope

A Dinosaur ABC

A is for Apatosaurus, head up in the skies.
B's for Brachiosaurus, of an even vaster size.
C is for the Crashing of bony dino heads.
D is for Dinosaurs. Are they all dead?
E is for Extinction. Did a meteor do it?
F is for Fossil. Don't let the dog chew it.
G's for Gigantic, like the great seismosaurs.
H for Horrific, tyrannosaurs' jaws.
I is for Ichthysaurus, king of the sea.
J's for Janenschia, tall as a tree…
K's for Kentosaurus, back all spined and plated.
L's for Loch Ness, still plesiosaur rated.
M is for Monsters. Where can you see 'em?
N is for Natural History Museum.
O is Oviraptor, who had long, swift, hind legs.
P's for Proceratops with its huge nests of eggs.
Q's for Quetzacoatlus, giant of the air.
R for Red Deer River. You'll find fossils there.
S is for Seismosaurus, whose huge feet shook the ground.

T is for Triceratops, three horned, frilled and round.
U's for Ultrasaurus, its size in its name.
V's for Velociraptor of villainous fame.
W's for Wannanosaurus, a mini-dinosaur.
X is Xiasaurus, who lived long, long before.
Y's for Yangchuanosaurus. Try saying that fast.
Z, Zigongosaurus, who always comes last.

Marian Swinger

oi !

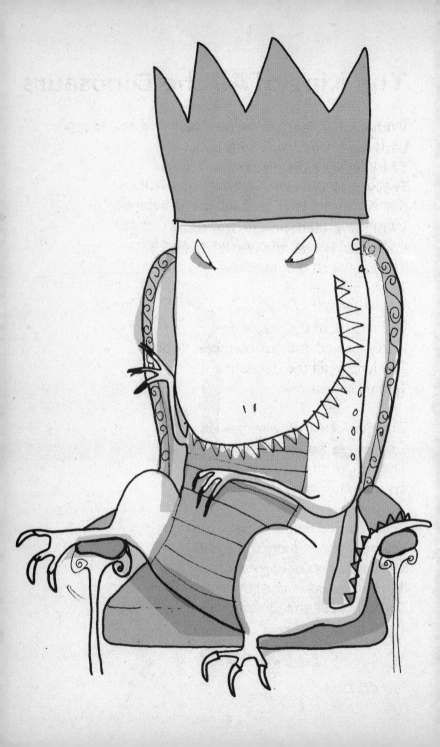

The King of All the Dinosaurs

With taloned feet and razor claws,
Leathery scales, monstrous jaws...
The king of all the dinosaurs
Tyrannosaurus rex.

With sabre teeth no one ignores,
It rants and raves and royally roars...
The king of all the dinosaurs
Tyrannosaurus rex.

The largest of the carnivores,
It stomps and chomps on forest floors...
The king of all the dinosaurs
Tyrannosaurus rex.

Charges forwards, waging wars,
Gouges, gorges, gashes, gores...
The king of all the dinosaurs
Tyrannosaurus rex.

With taloned feet and razor claws,
Leathery scales, monstrous jaws,
Sabre teeth no one ignores,
It rants and raves and royally roars...
The king of all the dinosaurs
Tyrannosaurus rex.

Paul Cookson

Ichthyosaur

An ichthyothaur
ith a dinothaur
that feedth on fith
and thwimth in the thea

Lynne Taylor

Iguanodon, Where Have You Gone?

Iguanodon, where have you gone?
You left without a parting,
I miss your crocodilian tail,
You left me sad and smarting!

Iguanodon, where have you gone?
It's true we'll sorely miss you.
They say you had a tortoise beak –
Even T-rex wouldn't kiss you!

Iguanodon, where have you gone?
A friendship blow we'll strike.
But don't ask me to shake your hand
And that fearsome knuckle spike!

Iguanodon, where have you gone?
You left a heart that's broken.
I'll never stroke your horse-like head,
Nor hear the sound you spoken!

John Rice

Tyrannosaurus Chicken

They say
I'm just a chicken.

They use my name
For cowards:

"You're chicken!"
they shout.

But I've just found out
Something really exciting.

The chicken on the next perch
Said, "Guess what!

WE ARE DESCENDED FROM DINOSAURS!"

I'm looking forward to when
The bloke who collects the eggs comes round.

We've got it all planned.
He's going to get

The biggest shock
Of his life!

David Orme

A T-rex's Disgrace is it Can't Reach its Laces

A T-rex's stride is fearsome.
Its legs are thick and mighty.
Its tail can knock a tree down.
Its jaws are big and bitey.

And yet you'll see it whimper
(For T-rex has the blues).
Its arms are *teensy-weensy*
And it cannot tie its shoes!

Robert Scotellaro

The Brontosaurus's Brains (and Where he Keeps Them)

I'm a great big brontosaurus, me,
As big as any whale:
Quite huge around my middle bit,
But thin at head and tail.

You might think I've a tiny brain
Inside my tiny head,
But half my brains aren't there at all.
They're somewhere else instead.

My secret is, I've got two brains.
I'll tell you where I've got 'em.
There's one brain tucked inside my head
And one down by my bottom.

So if you think I'm slightly dumb,
You'd better think again:
Where *you* have only got a bum,
I've got an extra brain.

David Bateman

Yum

Bum

Party Animal

Ankylosaurus
Hates to stay in,
He's just not
A shy kind of guy;
He much prefers
To go clubbing,
When you see his tail
You'll know why.

Andy Seed

yes

ouch!

What Colour?

Oh, its bones may be colossal,
But the trouble with a fossil
Is that it doesn't give a clue
As to the creature's actual hue.

Take that diplodocus fellow,
Was he green or blue or yellow?
And was Tyrannosaurus rex
Perhaps adorned with spots or checks?

And it may seem quite irrelevant,
But that prehistoric elephant –
The woolly mammoth – what d'you think,
Purple, puce or shocking pink?

Colin West

Terrible Lizards –
One to Ten

One big iguanodon gnashing sharp back teeth.
Two diplodocuses nibbling on a leaf.
Three fierce triceratops thundering like trains.
Four stegosauruses searching for their brains.
Five spinosauruses flapping thorny sails.
Six apatosauruses lashing whippy tails.
Seven seismosauruses stomping monstrous feet.
Eight oviraptors stealing eggs to eat.
Nine fine dimorphodons flying in a line.
Ten Tyrannosaurus rexes eating one to nine.

Celia Gentles

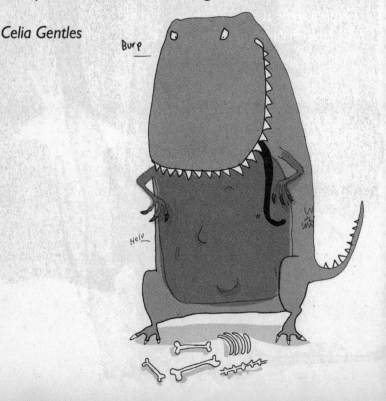

The Night Flight of the Pterodactyl

As I wait for the right current of air
A moonbeam glistens on my claw.

I take off from the highest mountain –
Not without grace,
Not without speed,
And with a spine of pride
Which tingles to my gleaming teeth –
I'm the largest creature to fly.

Gliding over the lake I make
A black shadow with my shape,
Warm blood pumps through my jaw.

I swoop on a sleeping frog,
Look up at the swarming stars,
Then end his dream with a snap.

Chrissie Gittins

If Dinos still Roamed the Earth...

Heavy Stuff

If dinosaurs were alive today
And we went to see them in zoos,
How would a diplodocus keeper
Manage to clean up their poos?

Lynne Taylor

Playing Games with Dinosaurs

Playing hide-and-seek with dinosaurs
Sounds like jolly fun,
But it isn't – I can tell you –
When the game has just begun.
When you shout "One, two, three, steady!"
And then "Ready, here I come!"
You will spot the dinosaur at once
By its huge round scaly bum.
While its head's stuck in a hidey-hole
Its rump's up in the air,
And a dinosaur's bottom
Can be seen from everywhere.
So play cricket with a dinosaur
Or tell it stories for a week,
But if you want a good time,
Don't play hide and seek…

Jan Dean

Snap! Crack!

SNAP! CRACK!
Munchety, munch!
Dino the dinosaur's
Having his lunch.

Run! Run!
Never look back –
Don't become Dino's
Next little snack.

Richard Caley

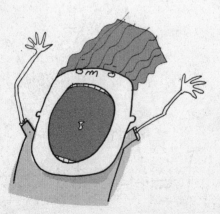

Dino Stars

Now dinosaurs are movie stars
They drive around in fancy cars
Blow smoke rings from big cigars
Their stomping grounds are trendy bars

They're the stars of every scene
Stare from every magazine
Moody, broody, cool and mean
Always on the silver screen

They're the big box office draws
Bigger than *Star Wars* and *Jaws*
The audience's biggest roars
Are for the film star dinosaurs

This is the land that time forgot
They're the hottest of the hot
Dinosaurs will never stop
Dino Stars always on top

Paul Cookson

Public Transport Solved

I wish that dinosaurs still lived,
I know what they could do –
Replace our transport system
'Cos it's useless through and through.

Arriving late, or not at all,
Dirty, cramped and slow –
But sit astride a dinosaur
And watch that dino go!

He'd always leave on time, of course,
And never would break down,
And never putter poisonous fumes
Polluting every town.

And think of what a view you'd get,
Perched up in the air –
Better than a double-deck
And only half the fare!

Tyrannosaurus rex – yes please,
And brontosaurus too,
Perched on top that big long neck –
Blimey, what a view.

Double-deck diplodocus,
Triceratopsy train,
And most exciting of them all –
A pterodactyl plane!

Yes, public forms of transport
Are all way past their best,
But if the dinosaurs came back
They'd get us out of this mess...

Clive Webster

Velociraptor Valentine

Dear Vicky V.,
This card's for you,

To show my love's both strong and true:

Let's hunt together,
Cause some hustle;
Scare herbivores
And flex some muscle…

I may not have enormous jaws,
But they are always, ever yours.

Mike Johnson

Rex T's Wreckers Yard

Get your motors mangled
Get your sidecars scrunched
Get your cycles shattered
Get your caravans crunched
Get your bonnets buckled
Get your tractors trashed
Get your lorries levelled
Get your buses bashed

Bring your scrap from yesteryear
Riddled, rotten rust
We can batter it, bend and flatten it
Pummel it into dust

Bring your metal, we can move it
We can squash it, crush it, cube it
No truck is too much and no car is too hard
Scaly tails swing and smash 'em
Stomping feet and claws that crash 'em
Metal munching megamouths at Rex T's Wreckers Yard!

Paul Cookson

Prehistoric Rock

Look at that band
On *Top of the Pops*,
Blasting out prehistoric rock.

They let rip,
Roll, rattle and shake it.
They won't mime,
They refuse to fake it.

And those costumes they're wearing
Aren't costumes at all,
What you're seeing
Is natural.

They may not be pretty
And they're not slick,
But they're racing up the charts
Double-quick!

So if you think they're a joke
And you're ready to mock,
Prepare yourself
For a great big shock.

Filling the screen,
Getting applause,
It's the one and only –
They're not phoney –
Let's hear it for ... The Dinosaurs!

Bernard Young

JOBFINDER

NOW RECRUITING
Express Parcel Deliveries

Suit Gallimimus with 2 years' experience and clean licence.

email: fastlegs@epd.co.uk

WANTED
for fish and chip shop
Baryonx for part-time
work (evenings 6 – 11p.m.)
Remuneration – free fish.
Contact Mrs Spears at
Snappers, Water Street.

Local club seeks
GLIDING INSTRUCTOR
(Advanced Certificate)
Pteranodon preferred.

Apply in writing to:
Mr A. Lightbody, Wingsover Airfield.

Nursery Nurse
MAIASAURA
(Level 2) required
to assist in small
family-run nursery.
Forward your CV to
Mrs B. Kind,
The Nest, Sandy Lane.

ATTENTION ALL VELOCIRAPTORS
Beauty clinic currently has
vacancy for a full-time

NAIL TECHNICIAN
Apply online at www.lovelylizards.com

LOOKING FOR A CHALLENGE?
Elasmosaurus needed on
expedition to locate
Loch Ness Monster. Able
to work as part of team.
Must be flexible.
INTERESTED?
Then come along to our
Open Day at Lakeside on Sunday.

— och
och aye

Sue Cowling

31

Dinosaurs are Everywhere

Dinosaurs are everywhere,
Every worktop, every chair.
In the hospital, in the street,
Stomping round on huge feet.

Dinosaurs in the cars,
Dinosaurs in the bars,
Dinosaurs on the floor,
Dinosaurs at the door.

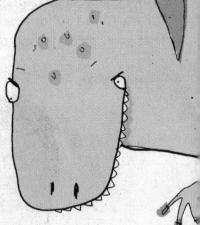

Stomp, stomp dinosaurs,
Big, big dinosaurs,
Huge round dinosaurs,
Everywhere are dinosaurs.

Dinosaurs all around –
Dinosaurs are there,
Dinosaurs are here.
So come round if you dare.

Don't come here,
Dinosaurs are near.
Meateaters, planteaters,
Dinosaurs are here!

Jade Wake
Aged 11

Prehistoric Pets

I'd Like to Pat Apatosaurus

I'd like to pat apatosaurus
But they lived so long before us
That you can't find one to pat.

So that's that.

Philip Burton

Dinosaur Warning

A dinosaur's a lovely pet
But never take one to the vet.

Vets use needles sharp as spikes,
This a dinosaur dislikes.

A dinosaur just will not let
Its skin be punctured by a vet.

A vet's inspection of infection
Means a selection of injections,
This won't meet with great affection;
Your dinosaur, with his collection
Of giant teeth, will wreck a section
Of the vet's neck – a real rejection
Of this medical correction.

(This causes vets deep dejection,
They are demanding some protection:
Sets of laws against the claws
Of upset, fed-up dinosaurs.)

So if your dinosaur is ill,
Phone the chemist for a pill.

Buy a lotion or a plaster
And avoid a real disaster.

David Harmer

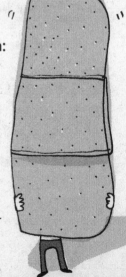

Petty Problems

Bronto seems to think it's fun
To take my sister for a run;

Steggie burps and WON'T say "Pardon"
As he chews his way through next-door's garden;

And Rex's appetite alone
Could eat us out of house and home.

The neighbours have all moved away –
The ASBOs will be served today –

And it isn't easy getting vets
When you have *dinosaurs* as pets.

Trevor Harvey

Poor Little Thing

A diddy little dinosaur
Was hiding in our garden.
He said, "Can I please be your pet?"
And I said, "Beg your pardon?"

He said, "I'm awfully lonely,"
He was very close to tears.
"I haven't had someone to love
For sixty million years…"

Clive Webster

Extinction

There was a young girl called Dolores
Who longed for her own brontosaurus,
So she went back in time,
Met T-rex in his prime,
Now, sadly, Delores no more is.

Karen Costello-McFeat

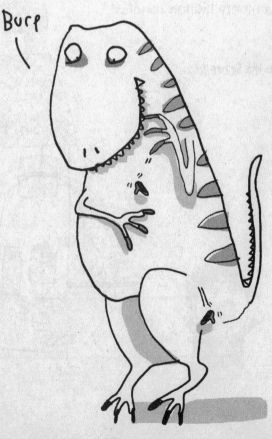

My Pet Dino's Birthday

Quick, go call the fire brigade,
'Cause my pet dinosaur
Is one year older and my friends
Are screaming out the door.

Our dining room is WAY too bright
And MUCH too hot to handle,
For on my dino's birthday cake
Are ninety million candles!

Robert Scotellaro

Short Dinosaur Poem

Behold the mighty dinosaur,
Jurassic or Cretaceous!
To keep one as a pet
You'd need somewhere big and spacious.

But my dinosaurs at home
Are safer and less drastic,
Being two inches long
And made out of plastic.

David Bateman

T.RX TXT

Txtg insd T.rx
R L8 vternrian

Sd I 10d 2 4gt
T.rx Rnt vgetrian

Texting inside T-rex,
Our late veterinarian

Said "I tend to forget
T-rex aren't vegetarian."

Mike Johnson

Dinosaurs
Don't Make the Best Pets

My dinosaur's
Been bad.
Mum's cross
It ate my dad.

It was wrong,
Mum feels,
To have a snack
Between meals.

John Mills

Dinomate

It's hard if a dinosaur is your friend,
Your problems never seem to end –

To cram him in the car is an awful squeeze,
He seems to be all tail and knees.
He steams up the windows and dents the door
And the air-freshener just can't cope any more.

It's hard with a dinosaur at your school,
He won't obey a single rule –

He thunders and stomps down corridors,
He eats his dinner and then eats yours.
In lessons he won't pay attention
And Miss can't keep him in detention.

It's hard with a dinosaur on your team,
To watch him play games is a scream –

When he kicks a football his claws go through it,
Give him a bat and he's apt to chew it.
He's rubbish in goal and poor at tennis
And with a volleyball he's a menace.

It's hard with a dinosaur hanging around,
It's hard with a dinosaur in your town,
It's hard with a dinosaur for a mate …
But on the other hand – it's great!

Laura Sheridan

Nursery Rhyme

I had a little T-rex
Nothing would it eat
But a chocolate biscuit
And my Uncle Pete

It chased my Auntie Emma
You should have heard her shout
And it didn't like my granny
In fact, it spat her out

Roger Stevens

My Pet Dinosaur

My pet dinosaur's back is bumpy,
And some days he wakes up far too grumpy.
His skin is rough, his legs are tough.
He weighs a ton, he is lots of fun.

My pet dinosaur's skin is green,
But it is extremely clean.
He likes to eat colourful flowers
And I think he possesses magic powers!

Amy Garner and Rebecca Gardner
Aged 9

Party Animals

Big is Beautiful

If lady dinosaurs shopped for undies
In department stores,
A style with extra curves in mind
Would have to be designed:
A whopping super giant size,
With sequins that would flicker,
And ribboned bows and girlie frills
On dino-tastic knickers.

Lynne Taylor

Today is my Dinosaur's Birthday

Today is my dinosaur's birthday –
I didn't sleep last night;
I had a bad foreboding,
And woke up with a fright.
My heart has started racing,
My stomach's in a knot,
I'm full of trepidation,
My nerves are almost shot.
I'm far too agitated,
My mood is one of dread.
Forget the celebrations –
I'd rather stay in bed.
Oh, today is my dinosaur's birthday –
I'm *so* down in the dumps –
I promised that today I'd give
My dinosaur *the bumps*!

Graham Denton

The Dino Dance of Death

Bow to my partner. She will curtsey.
(Ow! That massive horn thing hurts me.)
One foot forward, then the other.
(She reminds me of my brother.)

(Though I know that armour-plated
Skin like mine is very dated,
Her outfit is not exactly
Trendy – frills along her back!)

Turn around and then link tails.
(Watch out for those vicious scales.)
Turn again to face your partner.
Now we're all back at the start.

Roar to the left, roar to the right.
(A meteorite could come tonight.)
"One more waltz!" the others shout.
Then it comes and wipes us out.

Jill Townsend

Two Stegosaurus Discuss Beauty Treatments

"I've just had a waterfall shower.
Look at my scales,
I can't do a thing with them."

"For over an hour
I've been straightening my tail
Under rocks. And it's *still* curly."

"I tried the hot tar treatment,
It didn't take an inch of my thighs;
They're just as stumpy as they ever were."

"And as for the swamp sauna –
A complete failure!
My skin is still grey."

"Ow!"

"What is it?"

"I've broken a claw."

John Coldwell

Where the Carnosaurs Meet

Down in the forest, the carnosaurs meet
With a raging and roaring and thundering of feet.
Gnashing their teeth, they charge, barging and crashing,
Pushing and shoving, smashing and bashing.
They are there for a party, their manners are shocking,
With such snatching and grabbing the tables are rocking.
There is slurping and glugging and belching (so rude)
As the great, scaly monsters gobble their food.
Their eyes burn like fire, their fangs drip with gore,
As, thumping the table, they bellow for more.
After dinner they dance, an uproarious crowd,
Leaping and stamping and singing too loud,
Throwing rocks, knocking trees down
    (complete with their roots),
Splitting the air with their howls,
    shrieks and hoots.
And those who lope home through
    great jungles, uncharted,
Seem less than who went when
    festivities started.

Marian Swinger

burp

POP

Ten Dancing Dinosaurs

Ten dancing dinosaurs in a chorus line:
One fell and split her skirt, then there were nine.

Nine dancing dinosaurs at a village fête:
One was raffled as a prize, then there were eight.

Eight dancing dinosaurs on a pier in Devon:
One fell overboard, then there were seven.

Seven dancing dinosaurs performing magic tricks:
One did a vanishing act, then there were six.

Six dancing dinosaurs learning how to jive:
One got twisted in a knot, then there were five.

Five dancing dinosaurs gyrating on the floor:
One crashed through the floorboards, then there
    were four.

Four dancing dinosaurs waltzing in the sea:
A mermaid kidnapped one, then there were three.

Three dancing dinosaurs head-banging in a zoo:
One knocked himself out, then there were two.

Two dancing dinosaurs rocking round the sun:
One collapsed from sunstroke, then there was one.

One dancing dinosaur climbed aboard a plane,
Flew off to Alaska and was never seen again.

John Foster

Here Come the Dinosaurs

Here come the dinosaurs
Thud, thud, thud
From the deep, dark caves
In the deep, dark wood.

Here come the dinosaurs
Crunch, crunch, crunch,
Better not ask them
Home for lunch.

Here come the dinosaurs
Roar, roar, roar
Don't let them put their heads
Round your door.

Here come the dinosaurs
Prance, prance, prance
Kicking up their legs
In a disco dance.

Here come the dinosaurs
Thump, thump, thump
Tickle their tails
And away they jump!

Rita Ray

Come and See the Dinosaurs

Come and see the dinosaurs
Dancing in the street,
With bows upon their shiny claws
And glitter on their feet.

A little liposuction,
Lippy here and there,
With plaited tails and painted toes
And roses in their hair.

Dripping with perfumery
And skipping to and fro,
A dozen dainty dinosaurs
Putting on a show.

They've visited the beauty shop –
A rare and lovely treat –
And now they're happy dinosaurs,
Dancing in the street!

Bill Condon

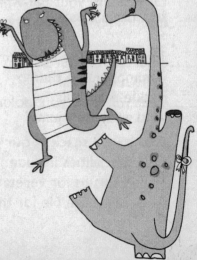

Di Knows What's
Best for Dinosaurs

Di knows what's best for dinosaurs.
For glistening scales and sharpened claws,
Visit *Di's 4 Dinosaurs*.

Whether you're two tons or ten tons,
Let our giant crane take the strain
And hoist you into our lake
For a refreshing dip.

Then visit our shower hall
For a steam-clean and power-scrub
Before enjoying a scale-polishing session
In our polishing parlour.

Sharpen up your claws and spikes
On our knife-grinding machines,
Or practise your tail-whipping
In our fully-equipped gym.

Smarten up your snarl
With a full facial
That will leave you looking grim and gruesome.

And have a snack in our gourmet café –
Our specialities include
Spiced shrubs for vegetarians
And mammoth pie for the meat-eater.

Di knows what's best for dinosaurs.
For glistening scales and sharpened claws,
Visit *Di's 4 Dinosaurs*.

A dinosaur, whatever their size,
Will never forget a visit to Di's!

John Foster

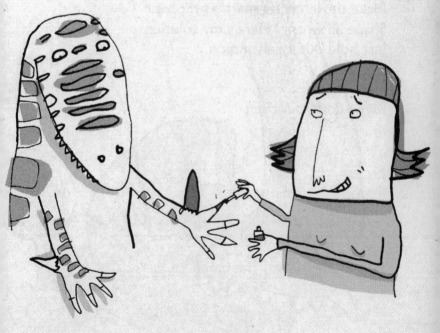

Fashion Feature

Ladies! Do you crave a mate?
These super tips will get a date.
The newest colours, straight from France,
Are sure to make guys take a chance.
Black is back as this year's classic
(Last season's blue is *so* Triassic).
Frills and long necks – sorry, they're out,
As is the ugly, duck-billed snout.
Accessorize with plates and horns,
Make those talons sharp as thorns.
Shape all wrong? Here's my solution:
Just hold out for evolution.

Karen Costello-McFeat

Jurassic School

Smellosaurus

I'd rather have a maths test
That's impossible to pass,
Then sit behind a dinosaur
With prehistoric gas!

Darren Sardelli

Sorry

We Want Our Lovely Teachers Back

In school today we had a surprise:
No usual teachers, all supplies.
Each teacher was a dinosaur!
Not a person to ignore!

The diplodocus
Began to focus
On scientific
Hocus-pocus.

The brontosaurus
Taught us a chorus
From his enormous
Hard-backed thesaurus.

The archaeopteryx
Taught flying tricks
From one fifteen
To half-past six.

The triceratops
Sang loud doo-wops.
Next week he's doing
Top of the Pops!

The megaraptor
Read us a chapter
From some dull book
That really grabbed her.

The iguanodon
Went on and on
A mad mathematical
Marathon.

I hope that soon they disappear,
Can't stand this dreadful stuff all year.
We want our normal teachers back –
Please give these monsters all the sack!

David Harmer

Ofstedosaurus

Teachers don't fear dinosaurs
or werewolves in the night.
They never fear the diplodocus
and things that spit
or fight.
They're brave, triumphant people,
they rarely shake
or quake ...
except when they hear
the noises
that ofsteds always make.

Peter Dixon

School League Table Results

"Oh dear," thought the Head.
"We're not that well placed,
I must think of a winning solution...

... I know! ... I will hire
a supply dinosaur
who can teach
all about evolution!"

Stewart Henderson

A Solution

Our teacher says it's a mystery
Why dinosaurs died long ago.
They just disappeared
After millions of years,
And why, we may well never know.

But I've got a theory about it –
They didn't just run out of breath,
Like us they had schools
With lessons and rules,
And the teachers just bored them to death...

Clive Webster

Reading Lesson

Class Six is reading silently
And it cannot be denied
That every single one of them
Is completely terrified.
None of them think they will survive
To the end of the next chapter –
Because their teacher is a mean
And hungry velociraptor.

John Coldwell

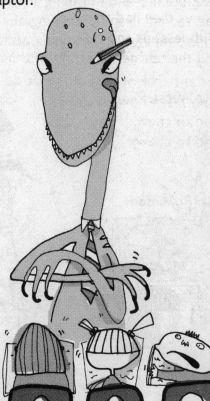

Dinosaur School

What do dinosaurs learn at carnivore school?
How to swagger and strut, how to cruise and be cool.
They learn gnashing and gashing and gnawing and clawing,
And lashing and dashing and roaring and warring,
And tearing and scaring and ripping and gripping,
And daring and glaring and nipping and flipping,
And chasing and racing and pacing and pulping,
And looming and booming and zooming and gulping,
And stomping and chomping, alarming and harming,
And stamping and champing, attack and disarming.

But at herbivore school what do dinosaurs do?
They learn how to chew,
And to chew,
And to chew.

Julia Rawlinson

Pterodactyl Primary:
a Summary Report by
School Inspector Brontosaur

Pupils: little pterrors
Head: a pain in the neck
Lesson plans: prehistoric
Teachers: all nervous rex

Jane Clarke

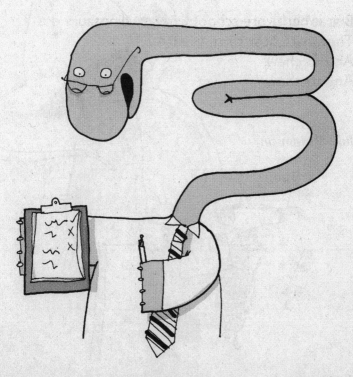

Prehistoric Professor

Those massive dinosaurs of old
Had very tiny brains –
Except the struthiomimus,
Who roamed the ancient plains.

He really was a dinosaur
Of notable distinction –
He took his dinosaur degree
And passed it with *extinction*…!

Clive Webster

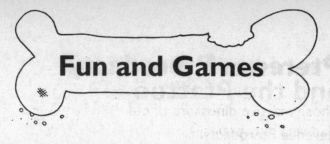
Never Play Football with a Stegosaur

Never play football with a stegosaur.
He'll kick you till your legs are sore.

Leo Aylen

Pterence Pterodactyl and the Ptattoo

Pterence Pterodactyl
Had a pterrible pto-do.
The pto-do was with his mother,
It was about a new ptattoo.

"Pterodactyls don't have ptattoos,"
Was his mother's point of view.
"I let you have one last ptime
And ptatty it looks ptoo."

My friends have more than one,
Thought Pterry, feeling blue;
Why can't Pterence Pterodactyl
Ptry ptwo ptatty ptattoos ptoo?

Ptrevor Millum

We are the Chompions!

We are the champs, we are the top
Of Premier Division One.
Nobody scores against us when
Our goalie is "Big Bron".

We're solid in defence
And cutting in attack,
Trexi's up the front
And Stego's at the back.

Terry D is on the wing,
Unchallenged in the air.
The midfield wins with the twins
Vel and Ossie Rapto there.

We play with incision,
We always leave our mark,
We're Dinosaurs United
And our ground's Jurassic Park.

Paul Cookson

Allosaurus Always Wins

Allosaurus wins at chequers.
Allosaurus wins at chess.
He's too tall for volleyball,
And still he'll beat you nonetheless.

Allosaurus wins at marbles,
Simon Says, and hide-and-seek.
He's the best at any test
On any day of the week.

When you challenge Allosaurus,
First he grunts, and then he grins.
Then he scowls, and then he growls,
And then he roars, and then he wins!

Eric Ode

Growls... Snap

OK

Parasaurolophus Plays

Blow those nose bones,
Honk and hoot,
Play those breathing tubes,
Toot! Toot!

Fill that hollow horn
With air.
When your skull is full
Then – blare!

In a band
Or on your own,
Sound that dinosaur
Trombone!

Sue Cowling

Bored to Death

No MP3s or DVDs,
No VCRs or DABs,
No mobile phones to text and chat,
Monopoly and games like that.
No TV shows with cops and crooks
No internet to surf – no books,
No big-screen films or video games,
No pantomimes with ugly dames,
No Rollerblades, skateboards or bikes,
No rigs with karaoke mikes,
No keyboards, drums or cool pop stars,
No drive-by-wire racing cars,
No making friends or hanging out,
No kicking empty cans about,
No shopping trips for fashion jeans,
No comic books or magazines.
No Lego or Meccano sets,
No superglue or Airfix jets,
No bright balloons or flying kites,
No Halloweens or Bonfire Nights,
No Saturdays or football teams,

No fizzy drinks or tall ice creams.
No candyfloss or lucky dips,
No pizzas, burgers, beans or chips,
No arcades or amusement parks,
No fireworks exploding sparks.
So – dinosaurs, it is my guess,
Became extinct from listlessness.

Philip Waddell

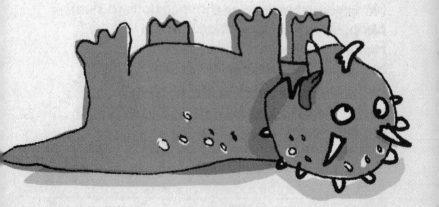

Cooking with Dinosaurs

It's seventy million years ago
And Diplodocus has had a tough day –
Now he's tidied his lair, put dusters away,
And he's ready to watch his favourite show:
There's nothing so good when you've done all your
  chores
As relaxing with *Cooking with Dinosaurs*!

It's top of the ratings on Jurassic TV,
When it's on there is silence in forest and swamp,
Not a roar or a scream or a rip or a chomp:
For who wants to miss this week's star recipe?
It's a much bigger hit that even Swamp Wars,
Yes, there's nothing like *Cooking with Dinosaurs*!

This week Stegosaurus is fixing a snack
(A vegetarian choice for those anxious to slim).
Chopping it up's no problem for him –
He's got all his cutlery fixed to his back.
So turn off the telephone, lock all your doors,
And curl up with *Cooking with Dinosaurs*!

Last week's show was a real disaster,
Tyrannosaurus was showing us paté on toast;
It began to go wrong when he minced up the host –
A carnivore can be a dangerous broadcaster.
But on plains and in mountains, on distant shores,
They still tune in to *Cooking with Dinosaurs*!

Another show's ended. Next week should be great:
The guest is a French archaeopteryx
Who's flown over to show us his secrets and tricks;
It's carcass au vin – I bet you can't wait!
So forget all the rest, watch the programme that
   scores,
The fabulous *Cooking with Dinosaurs!*

David Orme

A Dino Counting Game

One apato,
Two apato,
Three apatosaur.
Five apato,
Six apato,
Seven apato

ROAR!!!!

Eric Petrie

Acrobatic Brontosaurus

A brave brontosaurus named Fred
Decided to stand on his head.
But at thirty tons plus,
Twice as long as a bus,
He should have stayed upright instead.

Now the rest of the herd watched, and said
"We are all just as brave as old Fred."
So they copied his stunt
Upside down, back to front –
That's why all brontosauri are dead.

Alison Chisholm

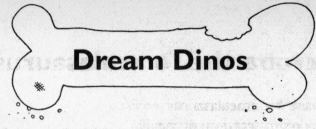

Dream Dinos

Dinosawwwwww

The dinosawwwwww has long, mean teeth
And claws that rip and slice,
And his zigzag tail saws people in two –
In fact, he's not at all nice!

Coral Rumble

Beware the Draculasaurus

Beware the draculasaurus
Who roams graveyards at night.
Don't let him grab you by the throat,
He's thirsty for a bite!

The other dinosaurs are dead.
Their bones have turned to stone.
Only draculasaurus lives –
A monster all alone.

His bloodshot eyes glow in the dark,
His fingernails are claws.
Beware his razor teeth.
Beware his slavering jaws.

As he lurks behind the tombstones,
The moon glints on each scale.
He's waiting there to wrap you up
In his forked serpent's tail.

Beware the draculasaurus
Who roams graveyards at night.
Don't let him grab you by the throat,
He's thirsty for a bite!

John Foster

Rhyme-osaur

Out of a deep dark mine-osaur
At roughly half-past nine-osaur
There came a sleepy steg-osaur
Into the warm sunshine-osaur
He warmed his chilly spine-osaur
Which made him feel divine-osaur
He nibbled on a pine-osaur
And drank a glass of wine-osaur
But then he saw a sign-osaur
Which made him yelp and whine-osaur
It forecast his decline-osaur
His time had come to die-nosaur

John Rice

Rubbish Dinosaur

I am a *Blue Peter* dinosaur,
I have buttons for my eyes,
A papier mâché belly
And yoghurt carton thighs.
My teeth are made of card,
My claws are made of plastic,
My tail can swish from side to side
(If you pull on the elastic).
But I cannot roar, I cannot walk,
I cannot pounce or bite –
They jiggled me from side to side
Under the studio light.
I'm painted green, to look the part
(And to cover up the writing),
But to be quite honest with you now,
My life is not exciting!

Coral Rumble

High Coo!
(A Haiku)

The skunkosaur died
An awfully long time before
It became ex-stinked

Philip Waddell

What's in a Name?

Zebrasaurus – black and white
Crocasaurus – bigger bite
Hyenasaurus – laughs a lot
Ponysaurus – loves to trot
Tigersaurus – stripes and claws
Sharkasaurus – lethal jaws
Doggysaurus – waggy tail
Snailasaurus – slimy trail
Hamstersaurus – cute and furry
Pussysaurus – warm and purry
Gorillasaurus – somewhat scary
Muskoxasaurus – awfully hairy
Lemmingsaurus – what a leap!
Sheepasaurus – not a peep
Addersaurus – hissy, hissy
Penguinsaurus – something's fishy

What's in a name?
We don't have brontosaurus
But we DO have his descendants …
So let's treasure them evermorus.

Andrea Shavick

Neversaurus

When dinosaurs roamed the earth,
So huge it was easy to spot 'em,
You'd frequently see a triceratops,
But never a tricerabottom.

Celia Warren

Thesaurus

This bookish little dinosaur
Of synonyms is king.
If you were to say *rope* to him,
He'd come right back with *string*.

I've tried to stump him once or twice
With something quite bizarre.
I shouted *fish* eggs at him once –
He countered, *caviar*.

Theo is friends with everyone,
But writers love him most.
He always finds the perfect word,
So they can catch the post.

He's still alive and well, you know,
Resting there on the shelf,
So why not dust him down a bit
And introduce yourself?

Karen Costello-McFeat

BIG H!

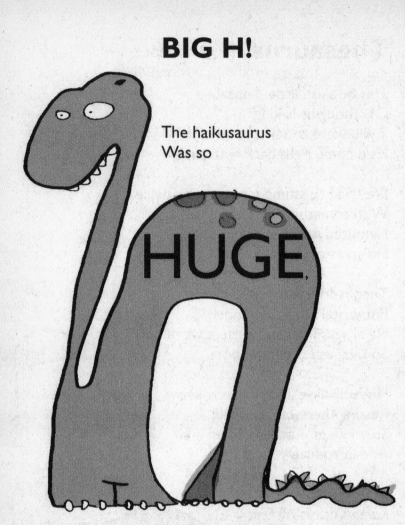

The haikusaurus
Was so

HUGE,

he barely squeezed

Into a poem

Graham Denton

Daisy's Dinosaurs

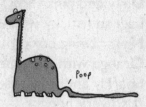

Bumposaurus – keeps falling down
Trumposaurus – makes a funny sound

Stickosaurus – made of glue
Knickersaurus – pink and blue

Spitosaurus – always spits
Sitosaurus – eats and sits

Lazytops – sleeps all day
Crazytops – dances all the way

Crockasaur – always croaks
Jokersaur – does funny jokes

Daisy Cookson
Aged 6

The Magical Diplohocuspocus

Dirty and pink
Icky and sticky, wearing a hat
Never being boring
Orange with pink spots
Sparkly and very sparky
Also very hungry
Using grass for food
Really useful!

Ella Searle
Aged 7

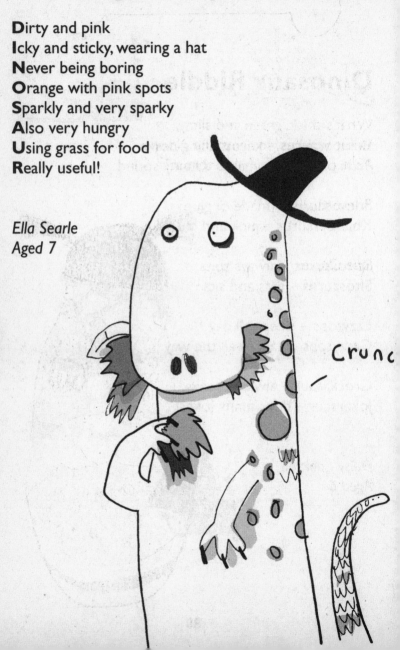

Crunc

Miscellaneousaurs

Dinosaur Riddle

What's thick, green and slimy,
What writhes, squirms and gloops
As it crawls down your throat?

Primordial soup.

Jane Clarke

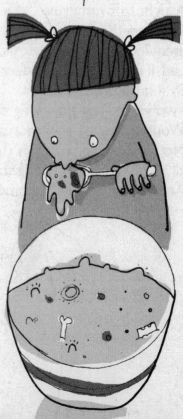

Slurp

Prontofaurus

I called to a halt our tiny band
Of time-travelling explaurus,
And now we crouched behind some rocks
Amazed at the scene befaurus.
Surely that majestic beast
Was the great tyrannosaurus
And there, close by, with thunderous cry
Lumbered a brontosaurus.
We rubbed our eyes – it was indeed
A sight to overaurus.
Just then they raised their mighty heads
In a blood-curdling chaurus,
Led, if my eyes did not deceive,
By a huge brachiosaurus.
I wondered just how long these beasts
Would continue to ignaurus...
No sooner had I had this thought
Than it was plain – they saurus!
And to our horror, in stampede,
Headed directly faurus.

It was their clear intention
To paurus and to claurus
And one horned monster obviously
Would surely try to gaurus.
"It would be wise, sir," one man breathed,
"At this point to withdraurus."
So, "Back to the chopper, folks!" I cried,
"Come on, it's prontofaurus!"
Safely aloft and much relieved,
We sipped cocoa to restaurus.

Eric Finney

Rhymes from the Dinosaur Nursery

Jack and Jill went out to grill
Dinosaurs deep in the jungle.
They barbecued one,
An iguanodon,
And for afters – archaeopteryx crumble.

Little Jack Horner
Had a small dinosaur, a
Stenonychosaurus.
They'd sing and they'd stamp
All day in the swamp,
And the pterosaurs joined in the chorus.

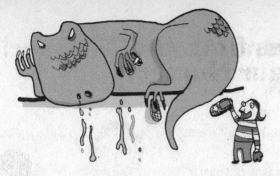

I had an allosaurus, much bigger than myself.
I put her in the greenhouse and kept her on a shelf.
I gave her a slipper for each of her twelve toes
And a cotton handkerchief to wipe her snotty nose.

Little Bo Peep bought a dinosaur, cheap,
But now she cannot spot the creature.
If she just looks behind,
She'll very soon find
Triceratops, ready to eat her.

Twinkle, twinkle, hadrosaur,
How I wonder what you were.
Just this footprint left behind,
Like the full stop to a line.

David Horner

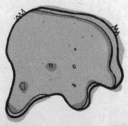

My Grandma is a Dinosaur!

My grandma is a dinosaur
She has a bony head
She has black hair, all messy

My grandma is a dinosaur
She has bumpy skin
All wrinkly and sweaty

My grandma is a dinosaur
She has a nostril on the top of her head
She has a mole that bubbles with death

My grandma is a dinosaur
She is extremely strong
The way she lifts the sofa with only one finger

Chelsie Teasdale
Aged 11

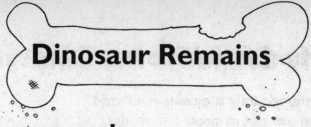

Dinosaur Remains

Photograph

A fossil's like a photograph
Developed in the rock
See?
A one-hundred-million-year-old smile

Roger Stevens

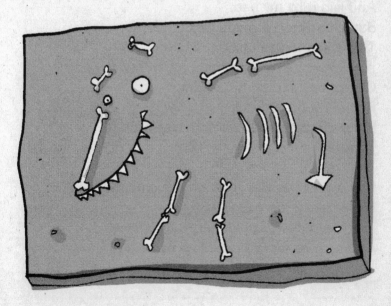

The Little Stone

I trudged along the dampened sand
With my pile of shells and stones,
A yellow bucket in my hand
Tugging at my weary bones.

I saw it there upon the ground,
Its markings grey and curled.
What a treasure I had found –
The best in all the world.

I brought it home that very night
And laid it by my bed,
But in the morning, what a fright!
There was a creature on my head.

Out of bed and up I reared,
Running with a shriek.
Who on this planet would have dared
To wake me from my sleep?

It was green as the grass on the emerald field,
Scaled like a mermaid's tail,
Teeth and claws could pierce any shield,
And its eyes were like yellow hail.

I reached out a finger that quivered and shook,
And touched the sandpaper chin.
With a snap and a crunch and a mischievous look
My finger was clasped in his grin!

Alice Markey
Aged 11

The Trade

I saw my buddy, Eddie,
On the other side of town.
He carried something lumpy.
It was bumpy. It was brown.

He said it came from dinosaurs.
He swore it was the truth.
I tried to figure what it was —
A bone? An egg? A tooth?

I asked him what he called it,
And he said, "It's coprolite."
I asked him if he'd sell it,
And he said to me, "I might."

I gave him my allowance
And a plastic model car,
A whistle and a wagon
And a spider in a jar,

My yo-yo and my bicycle,
My sweater and my hat,
A bucket full of comic books,
My brother's baseball bat,

My flippers and my slippers
And a broken tyre pump.
I gave him all the things I had.
He handed me the lump.

So now my buddy, Eddie,
Has the things I used to own,
And me, I have this lumpy chunk
Of prehistoric stone.

I wish he'd told me what it was
Or given me a clue.
I wish I'd known that coprolite
Is really dino-doo!

Eric Ode

Dinosaur Discovery

Locked in a rock
Left in the shade,
One dinosaur footprint,
Carefully made.

A picture of life
Hidden from view,
A time capsule opened –
One wonderful clue.

Locked in a rock
Deep down below,
One piece of a jigsaw
From so long ago.

A picture of life
Carefully made,
Locked in a rock
Left in the shade.

Andrew Collett

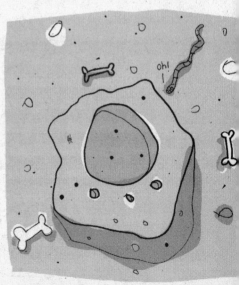

Dinosaur Museum

Sally was a herbivore
(or so the notice said),
a tail as long as lifelines
and a massive monster head.
People gasped with horror
as they wandered through the door,
for Sally was a skeleton
of the greatest herbivore.
Classes had to draw her
or write in little books,
others did a worksheet
or sometimes only looked…
Sally didn't mind them,
she didn't twitch a limb
to see the children staring
and making such a din…
But when a boy called Alfie
(a lad with little fear)
climbed upon her jawbone
and poked her in the ear…
Then:
Sally gave a bellow!!
She chewed him into four.
For unbeknown to experts*…
she was a carnivore!

Peter Dixon

*Palaeontologists

Claws (*Baryonx Walkeri*)

With my hook-like claws
I stuff my jaws
with fish snatched from the swamp.
I wade in the mud
that cools my blood,
then I champ and chew and chomp.

I boast a crocodile crest
and a scaly pink chest,
when fishing I'm a skilful winner.
I have a very long snout
that I poke about
round the insides of my dinner!

I have very sharp teeth,
a flat neck underneath,
I'm a slow-moving watcher and stalker.
I'm never in a hurry,
I lived in Surrey
and I was found by Mr Walker.

John Rice

Note: *Baryonx Walkeri* was
found in a clay-pit in Surrey by
William Walker, an amateur fossil
collector, in 1983. It has been named after
him but it has also earned the nickname
"Claws" because of its huge claw-bone,
which Mr Walker first spotted sticking
out of the clay.

Dinosaur Laugh

A statue of a velociraptor
Standing there so still,
With people staring in.

What they don't know
Is at night, when they're all asleep,
It runs around laughing,
Laughing at their feet.

Ferdy Boswell
Aged 8

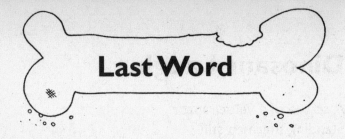

Last Word

The Last Dinosaur

I am the last dinosaur
you do not know me

you trap my footprints
you measure my wingspan
you weigh my last meal

but you do not know
these dreams I shared
    with sisters, brothers, cousins
in the caverns of our skulls

we dreamt the colours
    you have never seen
we sang the music
    you have never heard
we walked a world
    tasting air as clean
    as the trees
    which gave it birth

we left this world for you

   I am the last dinosaur
   you do not know me

who will you leave it to?

David Greygoose

Acknowledgements

The compiler and publisher would like to thank the following for permission to use copyright material in this collection. The publishers have made every effort to contact the copyright holders but there are a few cases where it has not been possible to do so. We would be grateful to hear from anyone who can enable us to contact them so that the omission can be corrected at the first opportunity.

Leo Aylen for "Never Play Football With a Stegosaur".
David Bateman for "The Brontosaurus's Brains (and Where He Keeps Them)" and "Short Dinosaur Poem".
Phililp Burton for "I'd Like to Pat Apatosaurus".
Ferdy Boswell for "Dinosaur Laugh".
Richard Caley for "Snap! Crack!".
Alison Chisholm for "Acrobatic Brontosaurus" © Alison Chisholm from *Ha Ha! 100 Poems to Make You Laugh*, pub. Macmillan, 2001.
Jane Clarke for "Dinosaur Riddle" and "Pterodactyl Primary: a Summary Report by School Inspector Brontosaur".
John Coldwell for "Reading Lesson" and "Two Stegosaurus Discuss Beauty Treatment".
Andrew Collett for "Dinosaur Discovery".
Bill Condon for "Come and See the Dinosaurs".
Paul Cookson for "Dino Stars", "The King of All the Dinosaurs", "Rex T's Wrecker's Yard" and "We are the Chompions!".
Daisy Cookson for "Daisy's Dinosaurs".
Wendy Cope for "The Dinosaurs".
Karen Costello-McFeat for "Extinction", "Fashion Feature" and "Thesaurus".

Sue Cowling for "Jobfinder" and "Parasaurolophus Plays".

Jan Dean for "Playing Games with Dinosaurs".

Graham Denton for "Big H!" and "Today is my Dinosaur's Birthday".

Peter Dixon for "Ofstedosaurus" and "Dinosaur Museum".

Eric Finney for "Prontofaurus".

John Foster for "Ten Dancing Dinosaurs" © John Foster from *Four O'Clock Friday*, pub. Oxford University Press, 1991, "Beware the Draculasaurus" and "Di Knows What's Best for Dinosaurs".

Rebecca Gardner and Amy Garner for "My Pet Dinosaur".

Celia Gentles for "Terrible Lizards – One to Ten".

Pam Gidney for "The A to Z of Dinosaurs" and "The Pterodactyl".

Chrissie Gittins for "The Night Flight of the Pterodactyl".

David Greygoose for "The Last Dinosaur".

David Harmer for "Dinosaur Warning" and "We Want our Lovely Teachers Back".

Trevor Harvey for "Petty Problems".

Stewart Henderson for "School League Table Results".

David Horner for "Rhymes from the Dinosaur Nursery".

Mike Johnson for "T.RX TXT" and "Velociraptor Valentine".

Alice Markey for "The Little Stone".

Trevor Millum for "Pterence Pterodactyl and the Ptattoo" © Trevor Millum from *Fiendishly Funny Poems*, ed. John Foster, pub. Harper Collins, 2004.

John Mills for "Dinosaurs Don't Make the Best Pets".

Eric Ode for "Allosaurus Always Wins" and "The Trade".

David Orme for "Tyrannosaurus Chicken" © David Orme from *Your Passing was Rubbish*, pub. Badger Publishing, 2002, and "Cooking with Dinosaurs".

Eric Petrie for "A Dino Counting Game".

Rita Ray for "Here Come the Dinosaurs".

Julia Rawlinson for "Dinosaur School".

John Rice for "Rhyme-osaur" and "Claws (*Baryonx Walkeri*)" both © John Rice from *Dreaming of Dinosaurs*, pub. Macmillan Children's Books, 1992, and "Iguanodon, Where Have You Gone?".

Coral Rumble for "Dinosawwwwww" and "Rubbish Dinosaur".

Darren Sardelli for "Smellosaurus".

Robert Scotellaro for "My Pet Dino's Birthday" and "A T-rex's Disgrace is it Can't Reach its Laces".

Ella Searle for "The Magical Diplohocuspocus".

Andy Seed for "Party Animal".

Andrea Shavick for "What's in a Name?".

Laura Sheridan for "Dino-mate".

Roger Stevens for "A Million Little Dinosaurs", "Nursery Rhyme", "Photograph" and "Watch Out!".

Marian Swinger for "A Dinosaur ABC" and "Where the Carnosaurs Meet".

Lynne Taylor for "Big is Beautiful", "Heavy Stuff" and "Ichthyosaur".

Chelsie Teasdale for "My Grandma is a Dinosaur!".

Jill Townsend for "The Dino Dance of Death".

Philip Waddell for "Bored to Death" and "High Coo! (A Haiku)".

Jade Wake for "Dinosaurs are Everywhere".

Celia Warren for "Neversaurus" © Celia Warren from *Penny Whistle Pete*, ed. David Orme, pub. Collins Educational, 1995.

Clive Webster for "A Solution" © Clive Webster from *Dinosaur Poems*, ed. John Foster and Korky Paul, pub. Oxford University Press, 1993 (poem originally entitled "Problem Solved"), "Poor Little Thing", "Prehistoric Professor" and "Public Transport Solved".

Colin West for "What Colour?".

Bernard Young for "Prehistoric Rock".

Look out for more fantastic poetry collections from Scholastic…

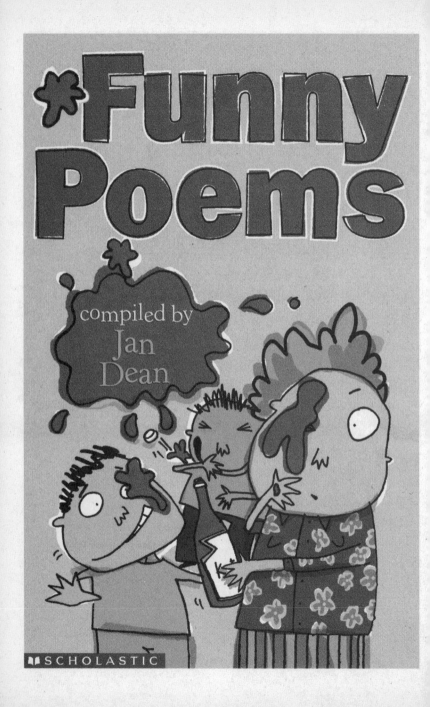

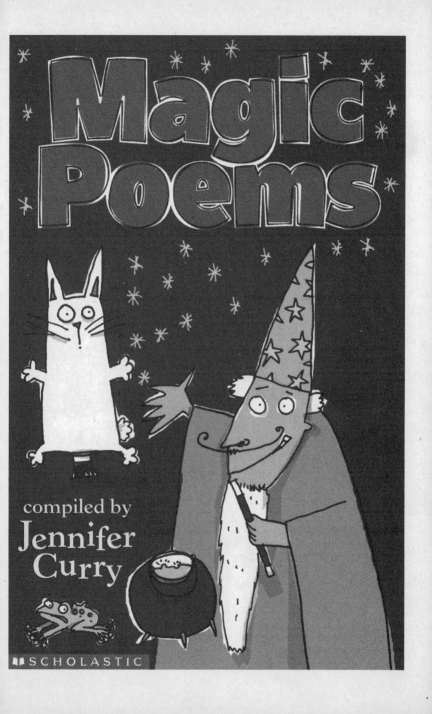